Neon Manila

Neon Manila
Troy Cabida

Nine
Arches
Press

Neon Manila
Troy Cabida

ISBN: 978-1-916760-30-1
ISBN: 978-1-916760-31-8

Copyright © Troy Cabida, 2025.
Cover artwork © Kulay Labitigan

All rights reserved. No part of this work may be reproduced, stored or transmitted in any form or by any means, graphic, electronic, recorded or mechanical, without the prior written permission of the publisher.

Troy Cabida has asserted his right under Section 77 of the Copyright, Designs and Patents Act 1988 to be identified as the author of this work.

First published October 2025 by:

Nine Arches Press
Studio 221, Zellig
Gibb Street, Deritend
Birmingham
B9 4AU
United Kingdom
www.ninearchespress.com

Printed in the United Kingdom on recycled paper by:
Imprint Digital

www.ninearchespress.com

Nine Arches Press is supported using public funding by Arts Council England.

Contents

Order No: #UK65388   11

Thalassophobia
A good boy   14
Sando   15
At the Mall   16
With both wrists silvered, watch me deflect   17
Ayaan bunks History and wanders into Art   18
You walked into school wearing your mother's heels   19
Empty Box of Calvins   20
House Poem   21
Brighton Beach   22
#nowplaying *Bloom* – Troye Sivan   23
Morning   24
No one wants what I want   25
Thalassophobia   26
race riots are currently on the way   28

Neon Manila   30

Disco Ball Unbreakable
slowed + reverb   40
Body Poem   41
Brown Boy with the Blonde Hair   42
Pearls in a Thumbprint Bowl   43
For the boy playing with silk scarves at 2:25am   44
Pussy-Bow Blouse   45
Cosplay   46
Say I am myself   47
Black Turtleneck Sonnet   48
Symmetric   49
Afterglow   50
Yellow Jacket I   51
Friends with Freudian Theory of Inversion   52

Elsa Peretti II, New York 1975	53
Desiring	54
Third	55
Yellow Jacket II	56
Not dying for London	57
Chanel No. 22	58

How to say no in Times New Roman, Size 12

On my first visit to Gay's The Word	60
You (derogatory)	61
My Daddy Baby	62
Citrine	63
They don't like hearing me talk about love	64
On Normativity	65
I invoke the spirit of Sarah Harris while shopping for my next pair of jeans	66

Bone Cuff	68

Acknowledgements and Thanks	72

"I want that red dress bad.
I want it to confirm
your worst fears about me,
to show you how little I care about you
or anything except what
I want"

– Kim Addonizio, "What Do Women Want?"

"for life
It is rather a determination not to be overwhelmed.

for work
The truth can only be recalled, never invented"

– Marilyn Monroe

Order No: #UK65388

The video advert IDs her as a creative professional:
jacket and trouser in biscuit, roll neck, canary,
caramel shades she rests easy behind. Through them,
she controls how much is seen, what can be accessed.
When she turns to stretch, exposing her jawline,
the light slides across the rims
like sun against skyscraper.
She is taller than she has ever been.
I wonder how much of her I could become.
If the exact pair will help
leave a trail of chic in my wake,
a breeze people will brush against
when I stroll past them out in the city,
white background permanent behind me.

Thalassophobia

A good boy

is proper and photogenic / has lived too charmed a life / does not flinch after a joke (other boys endure harder things) / searches for humour around the corner / stays until the laughter thins / is thankful to be alive / takes whatever is pushed into him / frowns through pain / makes way for the pleasure / enjoys the taste of cigarettes inside a man's mouth / comes with perfect moans / the perfect O shape / offers a hug when his top cries during sex / maintains good posture / lives inside someone else's trauma / out of politeness / comes straight from work to listen to you vent / boba in tow

Sando
from Tagalog – [noun] sleeveless undershirt

When they speak of the Second Coming
like all kids do on a Sunday afternoon,
they say Jesus will take you first
because you have always been easiest. You
who never pick at the santan flowers,
who never bothered to impress the girls
or size up to the boys. You
always with the plastic animals
while they practised kissing, swearing
inside abandoned houses.
They found you amusing,
their little pet, their question mark
chasing around the afternoon,
so unaware of your self, its lack of muscle,
straps of white undershirt
clinging to weightless shoulders.

At the Mall

Supreme quality, throws the saleslady's pitch:
material so strong it can even be used abroad.
My mother nods, eyes focused on the leather bag.
I watch her feel every button, each stitch,
run the gold-toned zip back and forth
before swinging it onto her shoulder,
handbag, crossbody.
I watch her imagine the hollow full
of small toiletries, phone, charger,
everyone's passports, the thickest jacket she had
laid flat on top for after the layover,
the jacket that will still be too thin once she lands
at Heathrow Terminal 2. British cold
welcoming her with a sharp, rush wind,
her shoulder firming the strain.

Both wrists silvered, watch me deflect
After Wonder Woman

teenage boy hate, drunk fathers, slurs
cold like bullets – I started this journey
in satin and gold vermeil, now I fly
in cracked leather and vintage Peretti.
I know this life is grand cinema.
Every part of my outfit is functional,
fashionable for my day job,
flexible enough to push back
the incoming tanks, the groping old men.
Despite all temptations, I've retired my sword,
lasso missiles back to the sky,
walk behind the explosion and smize.
I am all solution, empathy machine
in a boomerang tiara,
comic book scene at high noon,
the one untouchable archetype,
the one you cannot take home
and dismantle.

Ayaan bunks History and wanders into Art

In this specific lesson, Ayaan sits quietly
looking somewhat confused.
She sees the paint stained whiteboard,
the broken coloured pencils,
and half-finished Picasso impressions.
Nothing like the sterile, structured room
she's currently not in, all duplicate worksheets,
wooden tables facing one way forward.

Before the bell rings for lunch
Ayaan constructs the punchline
for a joke she will hold onto for years:
the irony in escaping one classroom
about white men and their opinions
only to find herself in another classroom
at the other end of school
learning about white men and their opinions
on how to express yourself.

You walked into school wearing your mother's heels

because your parents didn't have time
to buy a new pair, didn't know

excuse letters were allowed
in British schools. Coach Pudney knew

about the incident with the stolen shoes
but was too burnt out to do anything

so on the walk to assembly, you made do
with what you were given: the three inch heel,

pointy toe, all that shiny black leather
against the matte trouser material.

You walked past the kids, the teachers,
your cousin who ended up bullying you,

their heads like fluorescent bulbs
glowing with hate. When you get older

you will realise some of that
could have been guilt, shame

at the fact that they tried to
and yet you didn't trip once.

Empty Box of Calvins

I have never been alone like this before
hiding at the back of the house
next to the bins and the water tank,
all of them looking away.
It is so easy to believe nobody knows where I am,
holding a ripped open cardboard box.
The fabric contents now folded and safe
inside a drawer for later use,
the exterior I managed to salvage
features a headless cardboard man
with the chiselled torso
that survived the ripping apart.
The silence given to us
is getting thicker, generous,
pushing us closer to one another
until I start to feel flesh, hear voice.

House Poem

Sometimes I think about extracting
the part of my brain that makes men
look attractive enough to be wanted
to be taken home like a plastic trinket.
All I've ever wanted was a home
made of boulder and passion
where the marble will be spotless,
living flowers and summer fruit always,
where I can offer myself
the kind of tenderness
everyone keeps seeing in me.
Every room will be alit with sun
my loneliness will give
into the featherweight warm, slip
into small terracotta objects for display,
grief turned tactile, thus breakable.

Brighton Beach
"I had a perfect little life, it was clear"
  – Cecilia Knapp

We shook off the smallness of the morning
by being as loud as possible, inhaled the quiet cold,
gave it back in sprints across the pebbled beach.

We were young! Not much else was needed,
just the hard leather of a car seat
for a few hours' sleep, mileage still to spare.
We could have pissed right at the ocean,
our glittering youth all and forgiven.

After a bit of silence,
we let the jokes bubble up again,
waves approaching, retreating.
Punchlines about morning breath
and sea monsters, how we made rough
look attractive, ambivalence an aesthetic,
laughed hard to sweeten the slurs.
From afar, the four of us looked like true friends,
four anomalies that fit, actors
in a music video about eternal love,
the chorus sugary on our lips.

When they caught wind of our adventures,
the aunties called us makakapal, mga hindi na nahiya.
Wasting gas to drive somewhere no one knows you
with people who know you just to look at stars!

#nowplaying *Bloom* – Troye Sivan

a friend officially enters his romantic era

I didn't know we could close our doors to searching

I think of the men I've wanted for myself

and remember　　　　　　only the parts they wanted for themselves

angel　　　　　baby　　　　　and agreeable

to be touched on the tube　　　　　　and no one believing the hurt

made me love them　　　　　until they found someone new

I found the joke in their invasion and laughed along

then was told I needed to stop　　chasing absent bodies

walked home late one night　　　to a stranger stopping me

declared the things he'll do to me　　　so hungry in hate

o 2018 Troye　　　　　bleached blonde patron saint of gay survival

how much do I save for myself

I never knew I had to　　　　　in the first place

Morning

A young schoolboy pedals his scooter
towards Northcote Road's suburban glitz.
Next to him is his father, a man roughly my age
wearing glasses similar to mine: Clubmaster,
thick rimmed and circular,
the impression of a firm opinion.
His hand is a neat cluster
of car keys, the child's book bag,
a fully charged phone
in case of emergency.
I am fully aware of the lump of my rucksack,
its contents: the charger, the toothbrush,
the t-shirt from last night's drink up
and how the entire time
his other hand is careful behind his son
gold glimpses of morning light reflecting
back at me through his wedding band.

No one wants what I want

I'm not as effervescent as I look online.
I slept with your husband.
I didn't have to question your existence,
you and the kids just showed up, a streak of light

on his phone he turned downwards
on the bedside table. Before he climbed in
he opened the hotel window
to let in the breeze, to dissipate the noise.

All of Russell Square could hear
everything he wanted to do to me,
the things he did, the things he couldn't.

My friends tell me to be ashamed
for cracking into your marriage. I say
the entire time I wasn't even myself:
I used a fake name, wore my gym trainers
and sex boxers. Told him *I've been naked all day*.
It was whoever that was that held him.

Thalassophobia

"Sa patagalan ng paghinga, sa 'kin kayo ay bibilibib"
— Gloc 9

The punishment involves
the grabbing of the head.
Cold water inside a deep basin.
Dunk, soak
the writhing boy
until the father declares him
clean.

*

What I saw underwater
I took as a promise.
In the end, I decided
I wanted more of this,
this blue plastic future.
The act of flipping violence
against itself.

*

I think about the sirena,
mermaids in the river
I was instructed never to go near.
Those child-eating monsters,
the stories I heard. My father says
bad people do bad things
because when you have a life worth living
people will want to hurt you
as a form of taking from you.

On a dry summer day
my father calls me a [redacted]
for the first time
after he hear my friends
call me a [redacted].
He says it's because
I can't shoot a ball
or kiss a girl to shut her up.
Because I never play
in the monsoon
like the other boys do.

*

I leave the lights on
as I walk out of my house.
Past the trees, the bored teenagers
the other drunk fathers
the other terrible superstitions. Instead,
I focus on the hand that will catch me
after I throw myself into the river.

race riots are currently on the way

to who knows where
at this point
the infographic keeps changing

my friend called me this morning
telling me to take care

we laugh   find the joke

we've not had to do this   since 2008

in front of me
sits the most attractive man on the tube

(of course he's white)   look

he's putting his hand behind his head

he looks so comfortable
I can make out his tattoos

*

Neon Manila

When you are not so quick to reveal
such details like your number, your real address,
your pangalan sa gabi, your name at night,
you come across challenging, come across coy
in a way that seems to work against you.

Your innocence constantly petted,
praised like an act you got right.
Foal-like when in comparison
to all that they are, all they have let
the world force them to become

that some days, you feel you cannot be gentle
without bouncing off of something so violent.

Joseph   the doctor next door touches your leg
as he asks you out on a date
everything he'll pay for so long as he tastes your sweet
yes   he says all Filipinos make wonderful caretakers
and his back has been hurting all week

then there's Justin online
who's looking for someone to experiment with
who's been talking to only you all day
because you're just the right balance
of sweet and flexible to fit into his straight guy fantasy

and then there's Jason
who's always on about porn, who calls you sweet
every time you mention Pablo or Cliff or Rhyheim
admires how your face remains soft
even after seeing so much hardness

Back on Grindr, a grey shape face
is *Looking for Chinese bot.*
3some near Battersea. Reply quick.
You think about deleting the app.
See if the weight of your phone lifts,
if the heat stops picking at your fingertips.

After the first date, J texts you to ask
if you're wearing your Speedos.
J assumes you own Speedos.
You send him a mirror selfie in boxers
and receive a simple "Thanks"
like you would a last-minute work email.

You screenshot poems from this manuscript
for feedback. He's a teacher, lover of the word.
He says he hates the amount of awful men
you've had to endure. He says
you make the violent read so beautifully.

On X (formerly Twitter), an American
recommends the Philippines
to a friend, also an American,
as a one-way ticket to go
from being a 4 to a real-life 9.
10 even, he says, if his eyes
are blue like something new
or green like something expensive,
the same green taxi drivers will see
as a sign to take the long way
and fatten up the meter
but that's okay, he says.
That's part of the experience.
In loss and being lost,
you find yourself.

Later, 4.1K tweets will disagree.
Before deleting said tweet,
the American will ask
what's wrong? Aren't all Filipinos
forgiving? Aren't they meant to be so
tolerant and hospitable?

Like clockwork every lunch break,
your colleague will come into the staffroom
demanding *Phillip-inoh food*
or else he'll have you deported.

Today, he cuts the hour in half
telling you about the time he backpacked Asia.
He remembers how the humidity agreed with him,
how humongous the geckos were,
how Angeles City was full of girls
all ages and demeanours
it's like being inside a candy store.

Before the second date, J texts you to ask
if you could wear anything
that isn't a turtleneck. He says
he finds your neck so arousing
the same way he finds your leg hair arousing
and wishes you wouldn't be so formal
about the way you dressed.

All of this to say
that you are their
Manila soaked in neon,
their club scene chaos
housed inside a porcelain doll
who can only carry so much.
Their man-cave metropolis
for when the wife and kids
taste like chewed-out gum,
their mornings hazy
with traffic and frantic,
their nights exhaling smoke.

You, angel of light,
promise of something more.

Disco Ball Unbreakable

slowed + reverb

we are all charge and physical

        we build our own warm   relief

in skin against skin against concrete   mouths

        taste like   cold air and wine

hands thawing   inside unzipped denim

        the boys outside the bar

in their mullets and leather jackets

cannot see us   from the main road

though we are clear

        from the camera

above the flats   capturing every moment

Body Poem

If he must be clothed, you prefer him
in the slouchy cream jumper,
heavy knit and angelic,
the one he wore dancing around at home
and yet you saw his muscles flow,
how gracefully his torso followed.

When he's too hard at work to play with you,
collar and tie up the neck, you can at least study
the sleeves rolled to his elbows. Posturing,
biceps and all, vanilla dry down
and mornings under a five o'clock shadow.

Although you hate to admit it, part of you is hoping
all of this will someday lead to
to being in bed still sweaty, eyes blued
chemically, and him saying   Oh! After all that sex

and unspoken power dynamics!
I want to, in the end, give my all to you,
you efficient, hardworking thing:
my dirty white secret,
my patient little plot twist.

Brown Boy with the Blonde Hair

Since getting his hair bleached
the brown boy thought things would only get
closer to beautiful from here, the burning sensation
enough of a sign. But recently
he can't help but notice several differences
in the way people respond to him,
a certain thickness forming in the air.
After sharing a recent microaggression at work,
how politics affects his body and his people,
they are quick to call him brave and relatable
truthfully explosive and *you should totally write about that*
referring to the beauty in his tragedy,
the box office potential of his armlessness.
The way they look at him
reminds him of young homeowners
shopping for living room decor,
his dashing blonde, brown boy self
on display, a once broken bowl
held together by strands of gold.

Pearls in a Thumbprint Bowl

I have finally mastered the currency of kindness
and I swear to never let it outsmart me again.
My morning routine includes fishing for silver
from a black glass bowl, its lip curved for the thumb.
Inside lays a string of pearls,
an albino creature I'll never wear again
so as to divest myself of the person
who gave them to me.
In the Holly Golightly stage of my survival
I navigate the hot cement in crisp white shirts
feed on free gold and champagne
from men who accept my English compliments
and well-rehearsed smiles,
VIP rooms and GIA-certified rocks.
Make sure to let them in just enough
flirt over my past, not crack
under heat like pearls do, instead come out
of every interaction in an attractive, milky daze.

For the boy playing with silk scarves at 2:25am

here's something to wear

       to wear around the neck
       to cover over your head and ears
       when boys who smell of tsiko
       come up to you with questions
       that sound like threats
       if you've ever needed
       to hide the throbbing
       of your temples after the surge
       of the homophobe who's not hating
       just playing devil's advocate   if you want to be
       a disturbance
       to the flock of boys
       you're downing whiskey with
       their silver chains the size of veins
       superficial on a pumped-up bicep

Pussy-bow Blouse

The brown Filipino boy
Instagram influencer
slips his brown boy body
inside a pussy-bow blouse.
He lets the silk melt into his skin
its shiny, see-through combo
and then the bow, tied neatly,
accentuates the grace of his neck.
He chooses the best angle,
types away a caption then Share.

In the comments section
his friends talk about
how satisfying it would be
to watch pink melt into red
how the silk would feel
between their teeth
as they rip apart his sleeves
like meat off a tender leg of beef.
They wait for him to laugh along
double tap a red heart
maybe pop an emoji.

Cosplay

"I existed triply: I occupied space. I moved toward the other...
and the evanescent other, hostile but not opaque, transparent,
not there, disappeared. Nausea..."
   – Frantz Fanon

The Filipino family on the tube are studying me,
my black trousers and knitwear so natural on my body now
I feel like I embody Lived-In Glamour,
Serious Poet, Didion for Celine.

They look like they want to say something.
I lower my music, wait for them to speak – they look like
my parents, pregnant at sixteen, married by seventeen,
in London with their teenage son forty years later.

Ma, Pinoy ba?   Parang hindi.
                                 Hindi iyan.

The body knows how to reject when an object stops belonging,
suddenly finds the material itchy, too hot to keep on.
A train screeches, stops. The crisp accent emits from the speakers.

I say I am myself

and you trace me back
to my all black uniform, my clean,

linear silhouette, so little texture
distracting from the flesh you say

I look less ethnic now
compared to that old photograph of myself:

seventeen in mismatched denim, London lights
glaringly new against my cheeks.

You say I transformed well,
as in transitioned well, as in melted

into myself well. Like the black cat
sauntering in and out of the living room, I'm so slick

I could rob jewels from under your nose
become a worldwide accomplishment,

smile through the sting, sing song
out of your every ignorance.

Black Turtleneck Sonnet

With my first ever credit card, I bought one the brand called
the Newman: a stylish, manly neck, heavy duty against the cold.
I call my favourite one the Monroe: warm, merino and thin
like second skin, my favourite black slip.
One winter I got tired of the elaborate and thought-through
so I bought three of the same piece, black lambswool I wore in rotation.
I sprayed perfume on the chest
enjoyed the consistent praise they gave me,
the kind of clean they made me feel.
My first cashmere was bought in haste, thought the fast pace
would make the purchase easier to forget.
I had sex with a stranger the first time I wore it.
The material was hot against my torso after putting it back on.
It felt like a returning, like desire close to my skin once again.

Symmetric

We have become one scent, one pillow
our breathing surface level
once again.
As he sleeps, I study his salty neck
the silver cross necklace
I wore when I entered his flat.
On the expanse of his chest
the pendant is a drop of mercury
spreading itself, less cross
and more symmetric of bone,
closer to skin than testament.
The act of removing
is to assume a new role: his
ready prey, subject only to him,
my neck open only for him.
I bought the pendant
with no intention of having it blessed –
look at how compassionate it already is.
Having bore witness of our love,
nameless and transactional
and yet it continues to absorb
heat. Mine then his,
no cold in between.

Afterglow

After a bumpy conversation
about my writing
and the competitive nature
of the software engineering industry
the tub finally warms.

You offer me a pump of body wash
and, as act of service,
I rub my palms together
and produce foam for you,
wipe your chest as if clearing fog.

Inside the rippling water
our legs tangled between one another
share the same kind of beige.
Earlier in bed you enjoyed
the more obvious contrast,
the power that gave you over me.

Now you break eye contact, pretend
you're not being touched,
scrub yourself where
the bubbles leave a wake
from my own doing, scrub
harder and harder until
your skin reaches a new kind of smooth,
the water never cooling.

Yellow Jacket I

His rugged jaw, makeshift wolf cut
defining the narrow of his face,
then the left hoop earring that says *casual hot,*
I always just look like this, yeah, sure.

And then there's how he manoeuvres himself
into the jacket, how his t-shirt lifts up just enough
to expose a trail, the flatness of a stomach.
The easy gay poetry of it all.
When I see the cropped fit landing better
on his frame, yellow sheen against his skin,
I joke about letting him have it instead.
Staff get discount, right? We laugh.
We're having such a great time.

In front of the slanted mirror, I feel the pockets
for depth, study the soft collar against your nape
cocooned in a canary kind of yellow,
an incessant, hopeful yellow.
I turn around and he's rearranging the new coats.
I have a cinema date in ten minutes, I say, asking for help.
He says he'll do his best to keep it behind for me.
He hopes to see me at the end of the day.

Friends with Freudian Theory of Inversion

(1) Deviations in Respect of the Sexual Object

The popular view of the sexual instinct remains so today
because many can't hear the noise in the silence, *the poetic fable*
that evolves according to its chosen host and context:
the original human beings were cut up into two halves—
man and woman approaching me outside the tapas place
hand in hand. They will listen to my latest dating stories
and lament how much harder it is for those *whose sexual object*
is not similar to those of their more Instagrammable friends,
perpetually punished for *having these 'contrary sexual feelings',*
or better, as being 'inverts'. They don't say it outright
of course, that wouldn't be politically tasteful, but later
while holding hands on the bus, they'll think about me
alone on the Jubilee Line, feel sorry and other vague desires
to do something, but will have *difficulties in establishing it precisely.*

Elsa Peretti II, New York 1975

I will repeat, Helmut was flabbergasted
when he saw me in the Halston piece.
In the other shots you can see better
my mother's Ferragamos, the diamonds
that look like drops of light from afar
and of course the bunny ears
to complete the number. But if you ask me
the best thing about that photograph
isn't the ears or the Marlboro hanging from my lip
but the tears on my fishnet stockings.
How you can see the spots of skin
some bigger than others
as if the camera captured parts of myself
growing in real time.

Desiring

```
the boundless clarity
                        I have finally matured out of my petty sadness.


of them. The crystal                        to watch me, to tell me


promise, the always
                                  when you're no longer around
perfect angle of them.


                                  when I mess up my English,
Radiant cut, bezel set,


your very own
                                                    even when
                          Even on cloudy morning commutes


constellation
of floating diamonds.

                                                like true belonging.
Freewill and all, let these stones                  on my neckline

            declare      I, too,     have sorted my life out, secure
```

Third

The cold feels refreshing
against what remains bare of our bodies,
now a symphony of scents.
We give each other notes, then laugh,
slings his arm around my shoulder
to change topic. The side of his torso
is soft, I didn't notice it then,
his hand encompassing
mine. This is all temporary, anyway,
so we wait for the cycling man
to blur past us before
we kiss, slower this time,
no one to tell us to focus.
I expect to taste him,
the other, back in his flat
cleaning up after
our mess: the spilled water,
the broken coffee table,
the wet doctor's notes,
the half empty bottles
secure in darkness all over again.

Yellow Jacket II

part of the warmth you feel is his
then a slight wetness
on one side of the inner lining
from his t-shirt still drying
from when a car turned
and splashed a puddle against
the side of his dom top torso
on the way to work

Not dying for London

not   as in inhales that climb up easy
           as in exhales that flow easy

dying   as in straight guys who still say gay to mean stupid
           as in Hilary Duff where are you now

for   as in by refusing your embrace it is myself I am protecting

London   as in plague island   as in a city trying to kill me
           as in a city trying to toughen me up   as in a city trying to kill me
                                                  as in a city failing

Chanel No. 22

student of haute couture perfumery
draped in tuberose and incense
firm against exploding flashbulbs
you are untouchable
in your signature fragrance
that smells of your mother's makeup

onlookers will say why can't they
just wear something simple
as in invisible   as in already dead   dear
good boy keeping face
please know
you wear it well   all of it well
make it look so light

**How to say no
in Times New Roman, Size 12**

On my first visit to Gay's The Word

I thought of my parents the entire time.
Not them now, of course.
It's their younger, sharper versions
that pounce on me whenever I find myself
somewhere new, how they taught me to be aware
of how physical I am, that I may be standing
on someone else's spot.
I'm staring at a bookshelf now but
I'm distracted by the thought
of how my father would react if he knew
that the son he called faulty
and tried to whip back into shape
using threats of my ankle tied to a tree branch
is currently looking at books
about boys liking boys
and nothing was niche about it
nothing was blasphemous.
Here, protest is not a disruption to peace
but synonymous with celebration.
Here, a Filipino boy can enjoy his brownness
captured in a photography book.
The accompanied caption talks of how being queer
has affected his experiences using dating apps.
He simply calls it an exercise in multi-tasking.

You (derogatory)

For Valentine's Day this year, I was told I give off
the impression of someone in a committed relationship.
Long-term and solid. Loverboy with accountability. Perhaps this is why
no one has ever bothered to cop me up, ever took me seriously
on Hinge chats and movie dates: *he's cheating on his boyfriend.*
I give off strong great friends with someone's mother energy,
great with his previously homophobic father vibes.
I'm so emotionally intelligent. Only clear communication can do that.
I'm always fresh back from someone's hometown.
Perhaps this is why I have so many couple friends,
how often they invite me for dinner at their warm and modern flats
in the greener corners of the city. They rarely show guilt or shame
for showing me the physical manifestations of their bond
because I know what it's like, I have all the same things.
Whenever we're out, they always accept that it's just me coming along
because you, my love, just happen to be away this weekend.
Stuck at work or a writing retreat somewhere in Scotland.
Everyone knows you exist, that you do a good job at being my lover,
you just couldn't make it tonight.

My Daddy Baby

O daddy – you telling me not to stand too close to your flat makes me feel like I'm fulfilling some kind of cinematic duty. The sight of you in your grey tracksuits is a healing balm for several parts of my adolescence. When you play big daddy to my baby boy, it's because I let you. When you order me to worship, my knees hard on your tiles, it's because I let you. When you rip open your work clothes, it's because you are my rugged 90s Ken doll in this therapeutic mess of a fantasy and you are playing your role very well, big daddy. When we walk past one another at the bus stop, you in your suit and brown shoes, I never look. O my daddy – when you try to catch my gaze, I carry on walking and forgive you of your temptations. When we go by your fake name the next time we meet, the next time, and the next after that, I feel like a gentleman maintaining one's modesty.

Citrine

Another argument with my dad ending
with me in hysterics.
Something about having two jobs
and still not enough to live on my own.
When losing a valid argument
Leos resort to theatrics to conceal
ugly things like incompetence.

That night was all about hiding bruises.
I slip into a silver ring, citrine cabochon cut.
Under the lamp, the fluidity of the stone
shows endless possibilities, like money,
like stability. In prayer, I stamp my fingerprint
on the solid halo and imagine.

At a party the following weekend, a friend sees the ring,
his belly a beer keg half full and sloshing.
Ano ba! Who knew you'd become
your very own sugar daddy, ha? Your very own crazy rich –

When he gets proper drunk, he calls me mayabang
for not divulging the price. Isn't that the manly thing to do?
To talk numbers and how much of it you own.
How dare I not have his problems, he says.
Kids getting rude, bills never-ending.
Says I remind him of his girlfriend
and how she never laughs at his jokes anymore.

They don't like hearing me talk about love

as an adjective, a doing thing, umbrella term
for a collection of actions fuelled by the desire
to maintain or better a chosen object.
They want it abstract, less concrete
to make the violence natural,
an overarching power structure
we cannot escape from – it was love! That's why
you thought it was okay to drop out of uni. That's why
you thought he'd love you in the end. That's why
you lit up those paper lanterns in the park
behind Hammersmith Hospital, June 2019
made them bloom skywards for the birthday girl
who promised to cheat on her long-term boyfriend for you.
This moment was shared with two of her friends,
one she called the gay slur behind his back, the other
she spoke so much shit about to the local dentist
who saw most Filipino families in the area
who will tell her mother when they bump into each other
at the Asian supermarket by Chepstow Road.
She will say   Uy, pasensiya na ha
I really didn't want to say anything.
I love your daughter so much
but I just have to let you know

On Normativity

Over wine, takeaway duck,
and nursery rhymes on YouTube
for the baby already asleep
a straight friend urges me
to reconsider children, the chaos of marriage.

How about your last name? Who will
bury your body when you die? It's impossible
to get a mortgage as a single person nowadays!

While making a face
of someone thinking about it
I savour the salt in my tongue,
think about the flat by the bridge
I'll buy with the virtues of my face.
When I die, I imagine an ex-lover
I'd become better friends with
will come to clear out my glassware
fold my clothes into neat towers.
Have my ashes forged into a diamond
set on a chain or a gold band
a setting so clean
I'll spend this next chapter of my life
flicking light at the still-living.

I invoke the spirit of Sarah Harris while shopping for my next pair of jeans

Everyone in Kensington High Street is too busy wearing out their poodles and Neverfulls that no one has noticed Biba has been gone for decades now. The upscale exhibit space that took over the building sells broomsticks for £150 a piece. It reminds me of diamonds and how it took only one strategy meeting in the 1940s for me to call them an investment for my emotional security. The floppy haired guy who works for the Waterstones nearby isn't in today. I was going to ask him out last Christmas but I'm scared I'll become Weird Poetry Guy on their work group chat. It feels kind of insidious seeing white people's faces on the cover of ethnic cookbooks, so I do right by my people and put a graphic novel in front of a hardback on pan-Asian cuisine. The lighting in the clothes shop next door makes my skin glow a complimentary kind of yellow, as if the changing room is trying to say I see your body and despite your thighs I can make you catalogue handsome. I hate myself for hating the way my body looks. Rachel Long says *I won't look like this forever. I don't even look like this now*. In the shop next next door the lighting is less cinematic but they know the optics between hugging and hiding. I buy two: Barbie blue denim in ankle length and slim. In another version of this day, I would still be in bed with a man-lover I barely know, no clothes in sight. In reality, I want to let out a guttural scream because everyone here thinks I'm an exchange student and therefore do not contain any human emotions. I buy myself a box of cookies.

*

Bone Cuff
After Hiro for Tiffany & Co., 1984

contoured gold gleaming
with light   you
who come from death
and have risen
to adorn death itself

take on the colour
of rot   turn it
into skin
soft with desire

rework the gauntlet
from weapon
to crystallised honey
fluid once again

Acknowledgements and Thanks

Many thanks to the journals and publishers who first published these poems or earlier versions of them, as follows:

'A good boy' in *Exiled Writers Ink*. 'Sando' in *Masculinity: An Anthology of Modern Voices* by Broken Sleep. 'At The Mall' is after 'At The Movies With My Mother' by Joseph Legaspi, and it was also featured in the group exhibition *House of Haberdash*, curated by Lottie McCrindell for the Torriano Meeting House. 'Ayaan bunks History and sits next to me in Art' published in *The Book of Bad Betties* by Bad Betty Press. 'House Poem' is after the photo series 'You Do So Much' by Elspeth Walker and Yasmeen Melius. 'Brighton Beach' in *berlin lit*. 'No one wants what I want' is after 'Inventory/Personal' by Sophia Georghiou and published in *And Other Poems*. 'Morning' published in *The Battersea Anthology*. 'Thalassophobia' in the *Poetry Birmingham Literary Journal*. 'race riots are currently on the way' in *& Change*. An earlier version of 'slowed + reverb' in *fourteen poems*. 'Brown Boy with the Blonde Hair' is after 'Woman with the Wet Hair' by Emily Wood. 'For the boy playing with silk scarves at 2:25am' in *Ink, Sweat, and Tears*. 'Symmetric', 'Elsa Peretti II, New York 1975', 'Citrine', 'Pearls in a Thumbprint Bowl', and 'Bone Cuff' in *Symmetric of Bone* from fourteen poems (2024). 'Afterglow' was first published in *Bi+ Lines: An Anthology of Contemporary Bi+ Poems* by fourteen poems. 'Friends with Freudian Theory of Inversion' and 'House Poem' in *Two Poems* by Pearl Home Records. 'Third' in Seaford Review. An earlier version of 'Not dying for London' was published in *War Dove* by Bad Betty Press and *SLAM! You're Gonna Wanna Hear This* by Pan MacMillan. 'My Daddy Baby' is after 'My Friend' by Luke Kennard and was published in *T'Art Mag*. 'On my first visit to Gay's The Word' in *bath magg*. 'I invoke the spirit of Sarah Harris while shopping for my next pair of jeans' borrows a line from 'Hotel Art, Barcelona' by Rachel Long from *My Darling from the Lions*.

Kim Addonizio quoted from 'What Do Women Want?' from *Wild Nights: New & Selected Poems* (Kim Addonizio; Bloodaxe, 2015). Marilyn Monroe quoted from *Fragments: Poems, Intimate Notes, Letters by Marilyn Monroe* (ed. Stanley Buchtal and Bernard Comment; Farrar, Straus and Giroux, 2010). 'Friends with Freudian Theory of Inversion' includes quotations from *Three Essays on the Theory of Sexuality* by Sigmund Freud (1905).

* * *

Neon Manila has been a project five years in the making, and what a time it's been. This collection would not exist without those who have given it their generosity and care.

To Jane Commane and Angela Hicken at Nine Arches Press for giving this collection its home, for being a part of this journey from the very beginning.

To Rachel Long: I'm so grateful to have developed this book so closely with you. You are, and will always be, an influence. Thank you for championing the space my poems take up.

To Jacob Sam-La Rose, for everything and ever since. To Nathalie Teitler for your mentorship. To Jake Wild Hall and Amy Acre at Bad Betty Press for propelling me to where I am today. To Ben Townley-Canning and fourteen poems for publishing earlier versions of several poems present in this collection, for being such a big part of my writing life.

To Kulay Labitigan for creating my book cover. To hack mystic, latekid, Justin de Guzman, Bump Kin, Mokuma, Riwa Saab, and Pearl Home Records for producing the spoken word album that accompanies this collection. To Lu Martins for creating the *Neon Manila* paper doll illustration. To Kurboi for producing my poetry "singles" cover art. To Gelo Lopez for producing the video for 'On Normativity'. To Ray Roberts for producing the video for 'My Daddy Baby'. To Pedro Younis for taking my portraits for this book.

To Kim Addonizio, Sanah Ahsan, Dale Booton, Helen Bowell, Jane Bracher, Jeremiah Brown, Lewis Buxton, Joe Carrick-Varty, Chen Chen, Jill Damatac, Peter deGraft Johnson, Oakley Flanagan, Sophia Georghiou, alice hiller, Sarah Howe, Clara-Læïla Laudette, Joseph Legaspi, Natalie Linh Bolderston, Lottie McCrindell, Cynthia Miller, David Nash, Oluwaseun Olayiwola, Joladé Olusanya, Naomi O'Toole, Stefano Palumbo, Pratyusha, Courtney Roberts, Peter Scalpello, Zahrah Sheikh, Maxine Sibhiwana, Yomi Ṣode, Louise Walker, Jack Westmore, and Jennifer Wong: for the various ways you have supported the making this book.

To Karima Qazi and Keera Lawrence at Tiffany & Co. for your brilliant cut sparkle.

To all my colleagues at the National Poetry Library, especially Sonia Hope, Nina Mingya Powles, Elspeth Walker, Emily Wood, and Will René. What a privilege to grow together as artists.

To the Ombao family: Tita Eden, Ate Jyds, Val, and CJ for being one of my safest spaces.

To Aira, GJ, and Angel, for the last twenty years and beyond.

To Fatima Omar, keeper of my heart, the warmth you exude.

To Poetry and Shaah: to Fahima Hersi, for your laughter. To Abdullahi Mohammed – I owe you tamagotchi! To Idil Abdullahi, my cinephile. To Ayaan Abdullahi: I am so much better of a person because of you and your very important friendship. To Neimo Askar, for showing me the radical good in writing poems about bubble tea, school memories, and as you would say – my boh-dee. All of this exists thanks to you.

To Aadi, Mischa, Claire, and Vaughn: permanent sources of light. To Ate Aia, Ate Michelle, and Ate Selene, for loving me unconditionally.

To my Mom and to my Dad, and the ways you hold me.